CW00406191

A LENTEN CAMINO

Published by
Redemptorist Publications

Wolf's Lane, Chawton,
Hampshire, GU34 3HQ

Tel. +44 (0)1420 88222,
Fax. +44 (0)1420 88805

Email rp@rpbooks.co.uk
www.rpbooks.co.uk

A registered charity limited by guarantee

Registered in England 03261721
Copyright © Redemptorist Publications 2022

First published February 2022
Revised publication February 2023

Text by Sr Janet Fearns FMDM
Design by Eliana Thompson

ISBN 978-0-85231-608-5

All rights reserved. No part of this publication may be
reproduced, stored in a retrieval system, or transmitted
in any form or by any means, electronic, mechanical,
photocopying, recording or otherwise, without prior
permission in writing from Redemptorist Publications.

The moral right of Janet Fearns to be identified as the
author of this work has been asserted in accordance with
the Copyright, Designs and Patents Act 1988.

A CIP catalogue record for this book is available from
the British Library.

Acknowledgements

Spanish Tourist Office
info.londres@tourspain.es
www.spain.info

Department of Promotion
Camino de Santiago
Tourism of Galicia
Xunta de Galicia

www.turismo.gal

The publisher gratefully acknowledges permission to use
the following copyright material: excerpts from the New
Revised Standard Version of the Bible: Anglicised Edition, ©
1989. 1995, Division of Christian Education of the National
Council of the Churches of Christ in the United States of
America. Used by permission. All rights reserved.

Images by Janet Fearns unless acknowledged otherwise.

Printed by 4edge Ltd,
Hockley, Essex, SS5 4AD

Janet Fearns FMDM

A LENTEN CAMINO

Make a Lenten pilgrimage of the heart
through daily reflections
based on the Camino Inglés to
Santiago de Compostela

redemptorist
p u b l i c a t i o n s

CONTENTS

FOREWORD

SANTIAGO DE COMPOSTELA
A LEGENDARY CITY, A UNIVERSAL DESTINATION

By Richard Rivera Armero, a long-time official guide to the Camino and its riches

Exactly how everything started, we will never know. Maybe this is the reason why the origins of the city of Santiago de Compostela have always been told by mixing information from the old documents and chronicles, and completing it with the help of stories passed down the generations in what we call the *tradition*. In this way a fantastic tale emerged in which we cannot separate the history from the legend, the certain from the wonderful. This happened because we know too little about those ancient times, and people needed to explain it all. The stories and legends came to fill in these gaps – or maybe they arose because the best way to express the extraordinary is an extraordinary tale.

Either way, the tradition says that one day a hermit named Paio, living where is now the city of Santiago, went for a walk into the woods. And there he came across the most amazing spectacle: a bright light glowing in the middle of the trees. At the same time, he could hear angels singing. He had stumbled upon the tomb of St James.

Maybe nothing much would have happened if the bishop, Theodemirus, hadn't "confirmed" the identity of the tomb and the king himself hadn't backed the discovery, but they did. In this way they started the creation of a sanctuary, the *Locus Sancti Iacobi* (the Place of Saint James). But above all, from the very beginning, this place caught people's minds and hearts. People from all social classes, from all over Christendom, felt the call of Santiago. Along the centuries this human flow had a deep influence in European history and, above all, created a particular "Jacobean" culture (Jacob = James), spanning architecture, music, literature, traditions, legends – and more. And, of course, let's not forget about its deep implications in economics and politics, among other key historical factors.

But for sure, the most obvious and marvellous Jacobean creation was the city of Santiago itself. In approximately AD 830, when the tomb was discovered, the area was deserted: neither a city nor a village stood there. Santiago de Compostela exists *because of* the pilgrimage. In this way the mausoleum of James was like a seed which, watered by this flow of pilgrims, germinated and developed until it became the handsome city which we all know and love. This is, maybe, the most beautiful legacy this pilgrimage has left us.

In fact, the city has never cut this particular umbilical cord which is the Camino, or we should say Caminos, in the plural. For centuries they have nurtured the city, bringing to it religious fervour, new ideas, culture and fame as well as trade and money. And it still does today.

Indeed, the Camino still brings pilgrims in their thousands to Santiago every single year, from all over the world.

But the current success of this pilgrimage should make us think: how is it possible that a thousand-year-old tradition still *moves* the people of our twenty-first century society? What has it to offer for having captivated peoples' hearts for centuries? There are, of course, many different answers to this question. But the only way to discover which ones apply to oneself is to embark on this amazing journey. To follow the steps of the millions of human beings who, through the centuries, have taken the same steps before us is to become one more link in this very long chain…

We will never be alone in this experience. We become a member of this community of people which, across the land and through the centuries, experienced the same questions we might have, the same anxieties and doubts. Each one of us is looking for our own answers. Maybe, like the hermit Paio, we are looking for that particular light, that special music, which would fill our hearts with warmth and hope as we become part of a thousand-year-old story.

Richard Rivera Armero
Historian and Official Tour Guide of Galicia
rriverarmero@hotmail.com
0034693247645

"Buen Camino"

"You'll find that the real Camino will only start when you return from Compostela." My colleague spoke from personal experience. Then, I understood her words with my head. Now, having spent time on the "English Way" to Compostela, I understand with my heart – and there's a difference.

Medieval pilgrims were pragmatic. A pilgrimage was risky, often taking years to complete and involving hunger, thirst, sickness, sleeping outdoors, difficult paths – and bandits. Before leaving home, with no guaranteed safe return, many wrote their will.

Each pilgrim had personal reasons for their journey. All major religions stress the importance of an inner journey towards a greater understanding of God and of self. A pilgrimage to a sacred place physically symbolises the voyage within the heart and mind. Even if unclear, a pilgrimage has meaning and purpose. It offers a pilgrim a chance to declutter their life and become a better person.

To a Christian, a pilgrimage is also a dialogue: Jesus and the pilgrim ask each other, "Who do you say I am?" and travel together towards an answer.

An iconic symbol represents many pilgrimage destinations. Pilgrims to Santiago carry a seashell in memory of St James the fisherman. It marks every Camino path, representing each person's physical and spiritual journey. Pilgrims and non-pilgrims alike daily wish the travellers "Buen Camino", hoping that they will have a good journey, not only as they head towards that day's destination, but also within their hearts. This greeting is also a blessing on a voyage extending beyond a bed and a meal.

That is why so many people, after visiting the cathedral in Compostela, walk for another four days to the rocky outcrop of Finisterre, overlooking the Atlantic Ocean.

Some abandon their boots as a tangible declaration of wanting, with transformed hearts, to take their first steps on a renewed journey through life. I didn't. Instead, a tiny pair of leather sandals, made during the pandemic by a shoemaker in Bruma, will remind me to make my daily Camino towards our amazing God.

It makes sense, doesn't it, to use the pilgrimage to Compostela as a theme for our annual journey through Lent towards Easter and the new life of the resurrection?

Buen Camino!

The English Way (Camino Inglés)

There are at least twelve distinct routes for pilgrims to follow to Compostela, a renowned place of pilgrimage since at least the eleventh century. So, for instance, there are the English, the French and the Portuguese Ways, but there are also several within Spain. The shortest path is from Sarria-Portomarín to Compostela, a "mere" 113km. The longest is from Seville, a journey of 968km.

The English Way has two possible routes: from A Coruña (73km) or from Ferrol (118km). Both date from medieval times when pilgrims travelled via existing trade routes between England and the Spanish ports of A Coruña and Ferrol. They could reach Compostela within a few days and be reasonably certain of a safe passage home. The French Way, potentially also convenient for pilgrims from England, was longer (760km) and meant travelling through the Pyrenees, where bandits were a constant hazard.

Sadly, the Reformation made pilgrimages from Britain very difficult so that the English Way fell into disuse until its modern revival.

Today, the two routes join in the town of Bruma and continue for a further 40km to Santiago de Compostela. Pilgrims must travel 100km by foot to be officially recognised as having walked the Camino, so that Ferrol is the preferred starting point for pilgrims following the English Way.

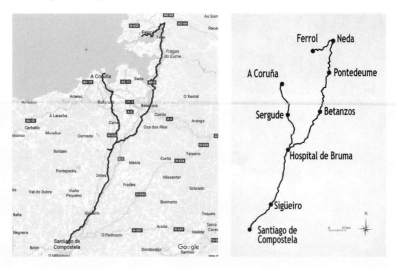

Santiago de Compostela

St James the Greater was one of the three apostles who appear to have been closest to Jesus: Peter, James and his brother John. According to tradition, following Pentecost, he travelled to Spain and spent nearly forty years there, preaching the Gospel. He apparently returned to Jerusalem, where he was beheaded on the orders of Herod, becoming the first of the apostles to die.

Various traditions, which can be traced back to at least the twelfth century, attempt to describe how the apostle's remains were transported from Jerusalem to Compostela. Whether or not the relics are those of St James, Compostela has been associated with him for more than a thousand years, making the site the third most important place of pilgrimage after the Holy Land and Rome.

Across the world, pilgrimage destinations are represented by an iconic symbol. St James was a fisherman and so pilgrims to Santiago de Compostela carry or wear a scallop shell on their journey.

The scallop shell is also traditionally associated with the baptism of Jesus, who walked to the river Jordan to meet John the Baptist, who is often artistically portrayed using a scallop shell to baptise his cousin. Thus the shell has become a uniquely Christian pilgrimage symbol.

The scallop is native to Galicia and so, in medieval times, pilgrims used the shell as proof that they had reached Compostela. It was practical insofar as the lightweight shell could be used as a convenient scoop for eating and drinking without adding to the weight of the luggage. It also acted as a measure for food distributed freely at churches and other stopping places on the Camino.

The scallop shell came to represent the entire pilgrimage – but there is a further significance, important because of its shape and structure. The ribs on the surface of the scallop shell converge towards a single point – as do the various Caminos, wherever the pilgrim starts their journey. The longest line on the shell traditionally points the pilgrim in the direction to be followed to reach their destination. In other words, the simple shell proclaimed that, through using it physically or spiritually, a pilgrim would be on the right road and couldn't get lost.

*Pilgrim shell
embedded
in the road,
Ferrol*

Our Lenten Camino

The following forty days of
reflection have a similar structure:
a brief description of a pilgrimage
place or feature is followed by a
photograph, a reflection from the
Gospel of the day and a prayer.

Ash Wednesday

A legend says that Hercules fought and killed the giant Geryon in a battle which lasted for three days and three nights. As a tribute to Geryon, Hercules ordered the construction of a city – A Coruña – on the site of their fight. He also buried the giant's head beneath the lighthouse which he built as a tribute to his defeated opponent.

The lighthouse, known as the Tower of Hercules, is the oldest in the world and has been in continuous operation since the arrival of the Romans in the second century BC.

Hence today, the coat of arms of A Coruña portrays the lighthouse and the skull and crossbones which represent Geryon's buried head. The city's ancient links to pilgrimage and Compostela are shown in the pilgrim's shells which border the insignia.

The English Way starts in the old quarter of A Coruña, at the twelfth-century Romanesque church, situated just over a mile from the lighthouse. The church includes not only some remains of the original second-century lighthouse, but also a sculpture of St James the pilgrim prepared for his journey. He carries a staff and a gourd of water, knowing that he must travel light, unsure where his journey will take him and what he will meet on his way. He will have to struggle against his own human weakness which will try to force him to abandon his journey when the going gets tough. He will need courage, determination – and faith – to keep on going.

Coat-of-arms, A Coruña (Above)

St James the Pilgrim, A Coruña (Below)

As Lent begins, have I the courage and strength to start my own Camino and to continue until Easter?

Gospel Reflection

But whenever you pray, go into your room
and shut the door and pray to your Father
who is in secret; and your Father who sees in
secret will reward you.

"And whenever you fast, do not look dismal,
like the hypocrites, for they disfigure their
faces so as to show others that they are
fasting. Truly I tell you, they have received
their reward.

But when you fast, put oil on your head and
wash your face, so that your fasting may be
seen not by others but by your Father who is
in secret; and your Father who sees in secret
will reward you."

Matthew 6:6. 16-18

Prayer

Lord, you know that I start my Lenten journey with many good
intentions. You and I also know that I will stumble along the way.
Perhaps the road will be rocky and I will stop to take a stone out
of my shoe. In theory, it means that I can be more comfortable in
reaching my destination, but perhaps I am simply afraid of taking
on too much and will take the easier way out. Help me, Lord, to
be a "good" pilgrim, one who will follow the path towards you
even when the going gets tough. Amen.

*Thursday after
Ash Wednesday*

AN UPHILL TREK?

Legend says that when Hercules defeated the giant Geryon after a lengthy battle, as a tribute Hercules constructed a tower above the buried head of his opponent.

Historically, the Romans who subsequently came to A Coruña found that the port's rocky coastline was incredibly dangerous for shipping. As always, the engineers thought of a solution and built a lighthouse on the traditional site of Hercules' construction. In the absence of electricity, a spiral track enabled wagons loaded with firewood to be drawn a further 34m above the 57m-high rock overlooking the sea to a brazier which could be kept burning to warn seafarers of the lethal underwater rocks.

Today's Tower of Hercules remains the world's oldest working lighthouse. It is a wonderful example of how thought, skill and sheer hard work saved countless lives over the centuries. Perhaps the waggoners had seen ships sink and witnessed the terror of those thrown overboard, perhaps unable to swim. Had some of them stood helplessly on the shore and watched the struggles of people whom they knew and loved? Whether the engineers, builders and waggoners were slaves or free, they had a purpose. Yes, the spiral path leading towards the fire was truly an uphill trek which they probably repeated several times each day – but it was life-saving. They journeyed towards the fire and the light it gave to people in need.

The Roman tower, showing the spiral path (Above)

The restored Tower of Hercules today (Below)

Might my life, unknowingly, be a beacon of light to others? Might my own struggles to overcome life's challenges reveal new possibilities? If Lent begins with good intentions which might not last, am I willing to start again if I stumble on the way?

Then he said to them all, "If any want to become my followers, let them deny themselves and take up their cross daily and follow me. For those who want to save their life will lose it, and those who lose their life for my sake will save it. What does it profit them if they gain the whole world, but lose or forfeit themselves?"

Luke 9:23-25

PRAYER

Lord, life can sometimes feel like an uphill struggle. "It is hard to be good". At the beginning of Lent, it feels as though I have a long way to go and yet you tell me that there's only one thing necessary: to be a loving person. Lord, when life is hard, please help me to try, try and try again. Help me to sort out my priorities. Be the light on my path. Help me to lighten the burdens of the people around me. Amen.

SIGNS OF PROMISE AND HOPE

Pilgrims who undertake any one of the Camino routes are guided by signs which point out the way ahead. The seashell and arrow make sure that pilgrims do not follow false tracks and get lost. When the road is straight, some signs are further apart from each other. When the route is more complicated, perhaps at a crossroads, the signs are closer together. Sometimes they appear unexpectedly, perhaps on the side of a building or at the edge of a field.

The stone monuments indicate their distance from Compostela, signs that the pilgrim's efforts to reach the city are bearing fruit and the iconic shrine is closer than it was at the previous milestone. The seashell suggests many roads – and many pilgrims – converging towards a single focal point. These milestones are, therefore, signs of promise and hope.

The milestone at A Coruña, starting the pilgrims on their Camino

What are some of the important signs of promise and hope in my life? Are there special moments when I know that I am heading in the right direction?

Then the disciples of John came to him, saying, "Why do we and the Pharisees fast often, but your disciples do not fast? "And Jesus said to them, "The wedding-guests cannot mourn as long as the bridegroom is with them, can they? The days will come when the bridegroom is taken from them, and then they will fast."

Matthew 9:14-15

PRAYER

Lord, you are my companion on my journey, showing me how to find you. I know and believe that you are in my heart but, Lord, someone once said that the longest journey in the world is the one between the head and the heart. Help me to see you, not in abstract ideas, but in the warm reality of the people whom I know and love. Help me to rejoice in your presence. Help me to love you with every step I take. Amen.

DAY 4:
Saturday after Ash Wednesday

Statue of the pregnant Mary, church of Santiago, A Coruña

BLESSING ON THE JOURNEY

She is beautiful! The twelfth-century church of Santiago is the oldest in the Spanish town of A Coruña. It is also at the very beginning of the English Way of the pilgrimage route to Compostela. There, in a tiny Lady Chapel, is an exquisite statue of Our Lady – and she is heavily pregnant. Mary's left hand rests on her abdomen in the same way that countless women throughout history have felt the movements of the little one in their womb. Mary feels the unborn Jesus and smiles.

Yet there is more. She raises her right hand in blessing. It's a wonderful example of folk art and theology "from the bottom up". Mary is in contact with her son and his blessing passes to us through his mother's hands.

This motif of Mary blessing us through her pregnancy is seen again and again throughout Galicia, in churches and on the sides of buildings. It survived despite official instructions to destroy such images. The male Church hierarchy sometimes felt uncomfortable with art which represented Mary's humanity in such a down-to-earth fashion. In Galician art, Mary is obviously several months pregnant. She is clearly in direct contact with her son in a way that every mother can recognise. She is a mother with mothers.

For pilgrims on the Camino, Mary blesses every step that they take. Do I allow her to be part of my journey through Lent towards Easter? Is she my companion, letting me feel her unwavering hope in the life that she carries within her? Do I let Jesus bless me through his mother?

GOSPEL REFLECTION

The Pharisees and their scribes were complaining to his disciples, saying, "Why do you eat and drink with tax-collectors and sinners?"

Jesus answered, "Those who are well have no need of a physician, but those who are sick; I have come to call not the righteous but sinners to repentance."

Luke 5:30-32

PRAYER

Loving Lord, you came into this world because your mother had the courage to say "Yes". She was willing to face the criticism of the people around her who didn't know or didn't care that she carried the hope for which they had longed, the blessing that God could become a helpless baby in our beautiful but fragile world. Bless me, Lord. Bless my family, friends and all those whom I know and love. Thank you for not expecting me to be perfect, but, with the help of your mother, may I become a little more willing to imitate her and say "Yes" to even the most unexpected requests that you are likely to make of me. Amen.

DAY 5:
First Sunday
of Lent

From conflict to hope

Was this one of the world's best examples of upcycling? What do you do with a castle which is no longer needed to defend a city from pirates, rebels and possible foreign invasion? Today, it can become a tourist attraction, but what if you want to do something different and use the strong walls, battlements and hard-to-equal location as a symbol of one of a global battle?

So it is that the fortress on the tiny island of Santa Cruz represents, not the fight with swords, bows and arrows, but one which, through learning, research and education, combats climate change and defends an exquisite maritime habitat. The struggle is still with conflicting ideologies, but it's in the interests of conservation, rewilding and developing a beautiful coastal walk around the island.

For pilgrims starting their Camino at A Coruña, it's impossible to miss Oleiros and the footbridge across the magnificent harbour to the tiny island dedicated to the Cross.

Monument celebrating the shearwater, Illa de Santa Cruz, Oleiros

Santa Cruz also celebrates the wild cinderella shearwater which, every afternoon for fifteen years, befriended the residents of, and visitors to, the island. The bird joined them, shared their food, listened to their stories and then flew away, to return the following day. Such was the shearwater's approachability and ability to bring people together, regardless of their origins, that she was created the island's Honorary Ambassador of Foreign Affairs.

Are there ways in which I can unite people in friendship and peace? Could I share their stories? Might I become one with our beautiful and fragile natural world? How can I nurture hope?

Year A "It is written, 'One does not live by bread alone, but by every word that comes from the mouth of God.'"

Matthew 4:4

Year B Now after John was arrested, Jesus came to Galilee proclaiming the good news of God and saying, "The time is fulfilled, and the kingdom of God has come near; repent, and believe in the good news."

Mark 1:14,15

Year C "It is written, one does not live by bread alone."

Luke 4:4

Castle of the Illa de Santa Cruz, Oleiros (Above)

View of the harbour from the Illa de Santa Cruz, Oleiros (Below)

PRAYER

Lord of life and hope, let me fight against any temptation to make myself the centre of my world. Let me look out towards others, to cherish them and build relationships. Let me defend the world which you created and made beautiful for my sake. Amen.

Day 6:
A castle or a pilgrim?

Monday of the first week of Lent

People build castles because they genuinely fear attack, whether the threat is real or imaginary. A castle is both defensive and protective of the people living within its walls.

In medieval days, castle builders needed huge sums of money and reliable supplies of building materials, transport, talented architects and engineers, cheap labour, land, a good defensive location – and patience. Few would-be castle builders had a ready stock of suitably cut stone adjacent to their chosen site so that stone-cutters and masons were needed long before walls and battlements could start to take shape. It took time to build a castle.

However, the beautiful harbour on the banks of the Ría de Ferrol also meant that Ferrol was vulnerable to attack. That's why it was described as "a city tanned in a thousand battles" – hence the decision to build strong defences. It explains why Ferrol's coat of arms shows its castle, banners, cannons and anchors: people were willing to fight and die to protect the interests of the townsfolk – and Spain itself.

Coat-of-arms, Ferrol (Above)

Castle of San Felipe, Ferrol (Below)

Ferrol is one of the two starting places of the Camino Inglés. It has often been described as the best natural port in Europe due to its excellent harbour so It's easy to understand why, in medieval times, merchant ships travelled backwards and forwards between England and Spain. It was almost as if the place invited pilgrims to go to Compostela.

Unlike castle builders, pilgrims travel light. They go beyond physical limits of time and space in search of a spiritual world which cannot be confined by mighty walls and imposing battlements. They don't need suits of armour and reliable weapons which can be used to bring about the downfall of other people. Pilgrims are movers, focusing on a different sort of stability to those whose primary interests are defence and protection. That's the unspoken reason why Ferrol is such a good starting place for a pilgrimage: it offers a tangible invitation to emerge from behind stone walls and to move towards different priorities and goals.

At the beginning of Lent, what is my greatest priority? Are there barriers which I need to remove and leave behind? Do I spend too much time defending myself and too little time reaching out to others?

A heart which is a castle is protective, defensive and, rightly or wrongly, can be afraid of attack. A pilgrim heart is on a journey which might sometimes be scary, but also recognises possibilities and challenges. A castle heart tries to preserve the status quo. A pilgrim heart is ready to change. Is my heart a castle or a pilgrim?

GOSPEL REFLECTION

Then the righteous will answer him, "Lord, when was it that we saw you hungry and gave you food, or thirsty and gave you something to drink? And when was it that we saw you a stranger and welcomed you, or naked and gave you clothing? And when was it that we saw you sick or in prison and visited you?" And the king will answer them, "Truly I tell you, just as you did it to one of the least of these who are members of my family, you did it to me."

Matthew 25:37-40

PRAYER

Lord, may my heart be vulnerable. May I know when to enfold others, helping them to feel safe and worth shielding, but may I also know when to step out and make changes. Amen.

Day 7:
Tuesday of the first week of Lent

Who is God for me?

What do you expect of your local Town Hall? Hopefully, you will find friendly people, ready and willing to help you and many others with the practical details of daily life: local transport, social services, roads, etc. You want it to be a place of reliability, listening, concern, compassion, support, efficiency: you can add your own desirable qualities to the list. It's no surprise, then, that architects across the world have tried to design buildings which enable local government to carry out its functions. Their work attempts to embody the qualities which the electorate expects as its entitlement.

Town Hall, Ferrol (Wikimedia)

The Town Hall in Ferrol is no exception. It's massive, decorative and firmly planted to one side of an impressive public square which is more than big enough for splendid civic functions and celebrations. It's a modern building but looks older.

Ferrol has been, for so many years, a naval stronghold, looking out to sea in the sure hope that it was almost impossible to blockade. However, because its focus was outwards, towards the sea, people living inwards, in Ferrol were almost forgotten and the town is now playing catch up, trying hard to provide amenities and attractions which will establish – or re-establish – life, energy, enthusiasm and homes. The Town Hall, therefore, remembers the past but looks to the future.

Most pilgrims are very aware of their life before setting out on their journey. They see that every step they take is towards a goal with God as its focus. They have started their pilgrimage knowing that it could be a life-changing event and, however scary that might be, they are ready to make those changes, one step at a time, for something which they know can only be better and more beautiful.

In today's Gospel, Jesus gives us the "Our Father" in which he presents God as our past, present and future, providing our needs for body and soul. God is not the "go to" in the sense we expect of a Town Hall, which can be a personal experience but can also teach us a great deal about bureaucracy.

Who is God for me? Who am I to God? Is God my infrastructure?

GOSPEL REFLECTION

"Pray then in this way:
Our Father in heaven,
    hallowed be your name.
Your kingdom come.
Your will be done,
    on earth as it is in heaven.
Give us this day our daily bread.
And forgive us our debts,
    as we also have forgiven our debtors.
And do not bring us to the time of trial,
    but rescue us from the evil one."

Matthew 6:9-13

PRAYER

Lord of my life,
be the Lord of
my love.
Amen.

Day 8: Where am I going?

Wednesday of the first week of Lent

Pilgrim shell embedded in the road, Ferrol

They are easily missed, these metal pilgrim shells embedded into the road in Ferrol. All it takes is for someone to be looking into a shop window, talking to a companion or simply thinking of something else. Yet miss this small pointer which shows pilgrims that they are on the right road and heading in the right direction, and it would be easy to divert and lose the way.

The shell itself must be thoughtfully observed because, without thinking, it's easy to retrace one's steps and travel backwards along a path which is already trodden and is now a thing of the past. The lines on the shell converge: they meet at Compostela. They represent many people, each making a different journey along their own Camino, yet united in purpose, wanting to reach their goal of the shrine of St James. Will some turn back before the vast cathedral comes into sight? Will some continue beyond Compostela to Finisterre and the ocean, the symbol of change and the first steps of a new life?

Where am I on my personal Camino through Lent? Do I sometimes fall by the wayside, lose sight of where I am heading and need to make a fresh start? Am I confidently following the signs, unerringly heading in the right direction? Where am I?

"The queen of the South... came from the ends of the earth to listen to the wisdom of Solomon, and see, something greater than Solomon is here!"

Luke 11:31

PRAYER

Make me know your ways, O Lord;
    teach me your paths.
Lead me in your truth, and teach me,
    for you are the God of my salvation;
    for you I wait all day long.

Psalm 25:4-5

DAY 9:
Thursday of the first week of Lent

FREEDOM TO BE THEMSELVES

Everybody needs a place where they can feel free, secure and cater for their most basic needs. Pilgrims are no exception.

The pilgrim hostel at Neda

That is why every route to Compostela, including the Camino Inglés, offers places of refuge where travellers can stay overnight on their journey. This tradition dates from medieval times, as is proved by the many remains of such places. Often, monastic communities cared for the pilgrims, sharing with them what they had in a typical gesture of monastic hospitality. Today, although religious communities are often associated with the shelters of many shapes and sizes, more often it is the laypeople who take on the responsibility.

An advantage of these pilgrim hostels is that people have space to talk, to share their experiences, to rest, tend their blisters and prepare for the next stage of their pilgrimage. A hostel is not the end of the road: it is a stage on the journey and an energising temporary respite.

Are there places in my life which act as a pilgrim hostel, allowing me to rediscover energy and enthusiasm, perhaps in the company of like-minded people? Are there places in my life which offer a safe place to share with others all that lies deep within my heart? Do I give others that freedom to be themselves?

"Ask, and it will be given you; search, and you will find; knock, and the door will be opened for you. For everyone who asks receives, and everyone who searches finds, and for everyone who knocks, the door will be opened."

Matthew 7:7-8

PRAYER

Lord, be my resting and my rising, my going out and coming home. Watch over, bless and protect everyone I know and love as we journey through life. Amen.

DAY 10:
Friday of the first
week of Lent

HELP MYSELF OR OTHERS?

A boar and a bear: what words spring to mind? Immense power, ferocity, strength, tenacity? The Andrade family didn't need to write a catalogue of their real or imagined qualities when they adopted a bear and a boar as their coat of arms. They had something else in their favour: a strong castle, extensive land, huge wealth – and a willingness to further increase their personal wealth and status through personal ingenuity and other people's hard work.

There was something else they could do. Living in a castle on the banks of the river Eume, the Andrade family needed to defend their lands and its inhabitants. They also needed access to traders and their livestock, produce and other goods. And so, in the thirteenth century, they built a wooden bridge and then, a century later, one of stone across the Eume. In fact, the bridge gave rise to the name of the town of Pontedeume (Eume Bridge).

*The Andrade Tower
(Above)*

*The Andrade bridge
(Below)*

Whoever controls the only bridge across a river into the town wields considerable power. It can be easily defended against advancing enemies – but it can also be used to extract tolls from travellers and merchants. Thus, the Andrade family soon became very wealthy and quickly showed the power of their authority by locating their coat of arms of the bear and the boar everywhere possible: nobody could forget Andrade importance.

Pontedeume has been associated with the English Way to Compostela since at least the early sixteenth century when Fernando de Andrade ordered the construction of the church of St James, where he is entombed.

As it was, the then Archbishop of Santiago de Compostela, Bartolomé Rajoi y Losada, was himself a native of Pontedeume. Did Andrade and the Archbishop want to highlight their birthplace and family home, but also to link it to the shrine of St James where the pilgrims were heading? What were their motives?

Put yourself in the shoes of a farmer who used the bridge to sell his vegetables in the market in Pontedeume. Was he pleased because, through the bridge, he had a secure means of supporting his family? Did he grumble because of the toll which lined the pockets of people who already had wealth beyond his imagining?

What aspects of my life help other people but are also calculated to help me even more? How might I nurture justice and equality?

GOSPEL REFLECTION

"When you are offering your gift at the altar, if you remember that your brother or sister has something against you, leave your gift there before the altar and go; first be reconciled to your brother or sister, and then come and offer your gift."

Matthew 5:23

PRAYER

Lord, help me not to let my good deeds help me more than they help others. Amen.

Remember me – how?

How do you want to be remembered when you die?

*Church of San
Francisco, Betanzos
(Wikipedia)*

Pilgrims visiting the church of San Francisco de Betanzos can't miss the tomb of Fernán Pérez, unmissably a member of the Andrade family. An impressive boar and a bear, the animals associated with the family and its coat of arms, carry his stone tomb on their backs. Its sides are notably absent of religious decoration, although a couple of angels carry his coat of arms at the head of the sarcophagus. Instead, hunting scenes decorate the sides of the tomb whilst his much-loved dogs surround the knight himself, as he lies in death.

There seem to have been two sides to Fernán Pérez de Andrade. He was a loyal knight and yet could switch sides to suit his pocket and influence. A builder of churches, he also appropriated Church property. He ordered the construction of the mighty 913m-long bridge of Pontedeume, with its seventy-nine arches, a twelve-bedded hospital and a chapel – and demanded tolls from those who crossed it, enriching his personal wealth at their expense. Described as "the Good", he is also remembered for abusive and unscrupulous behaviour in his search for wealth, power and influence. People are complex, aren't they?

How would I like people to remember me? What epitaph would I write for myself? How might others describe me?

"I say to you, love your enemies and pray
for those who persecute you, so that you
may be children of your Father in heaven; for
he makes his sun rise on the evil and on the
good, and sends rain on the righteous and on
the unrighteous."

Matthew 5:44-45

*Tomb of Fernán
Peres de Andrade*

PRAYER

Lord God, help me to be authentic in my journey towards
you. If I am sometimes confused and complicated, please
unconfuse and uncomplicate me. Amen.

MY UNIQUE PATH TO GOD

"**R**etire? Why should I retire? I love what I'm doing. I'm eighty-five years old and I've been making shoes all my life. My father and grandfather were shoemakers: there's their photo. During the Covid lockdown, I stayed busy by making miniature sandals. See: they're in the basket."

The elderly shoemaker, Betanzos (Above)

His miniature sandals (Below)

The elderly shoemaker in the town of Betanzos continued working whilst he talked, surrounded by shoes of every shape and size. His shop opened to the street so that he could see and be seen. How many pilgrims had stopped to greet him or had asked him to repair their footwear so that they could continue on their journey to Compostela? Some had later sent photos of him at his bench.

A craftsman to his fingertips, he had helped in the family business since childhood. "I didn't like going to school. I just wanted to make shoes. Now, I could stop work but I don't want to do so. I've taught my son to make shoes and he's teaching his children."

Each of us has a unique path to God. The shoemaker discovered his through leather and communicating with others through their need for comfortable feet. What helps me to feel close to God?

GOSPEL REFLECTION

Year A A voice from the cloud said, "This is my Son, the Beloved; with him I am well pleased; listen to him!"

Matthew 17:5

Year B Then a cloud overshadowed them, and from the cloud there came a voice, "This is my Son, the Beloved; listen to him!"

Mark 9:7

Year C Then from the cloud came a voice that said, "This is my Son, my Chosen; listen to him!"

Luke 9:35

PRAYER

Open my ears, Lord, to hear your voice in everything that I say, think and do. Amen.

HOW BRAVE AM I?

Unless it happens to be icy and the middle of winter, all of us can, from time to time, rejoice in taking a road which slopes downwards. Yes, we might need to be careful, but the road is often quicker and easier to follow.

A street in Betanzos

Some of the roads in Betanzos are very steep. They are colourful, beautifully decorated and a joy to investigate – but then, there's the need to return. The upward climb needs determination and the occasional stop for a breath. One can imagine boys and bicycles hurtling downwards whilst pedestrians fear for their lives, but even boys must push their bicycles uphill again. (Why are boys more likely than girls to take risks?)

What risks do I take in life, or do I prefer to take the safe path? When has God asked me to be brave?

"Do not judge, and you will not be judged;
do not condemn, and you will not be
condemned. Forgive, and you will be forgiven;
give, and it will be given to you."

Luke 6:37

PRAYER

Lord, please give me the courage and determination
I need to face life's ups and downs. Be with me in my
decision-making. Amen.

Tuesday of the second week of Lent

TODAY'S ESSENTIAL INGREDIENT

Life was so hard for so many people in nineteenth- century Spain that whole families emigrated to Argentina, sometimes depopulating entire villages. Often, it was the men who went in search of work, promising to send money to support their struggling wives and children. Sadly, some never returned and, once in the New World, began a new life. They left their wives as breadwinners who had little or no idea whether their husbands were dead or alive. Galicia was one Spanish region where families survived because of the tenacity and courage of the women.

However, just as today's migrants send a huge proportion of their income to their families to feed, clothe and educate them, the same thing happened with an uncounted number of those who emigrated to Argentina. Often, those who were able to earn a good income and even become wealthy, helped with the rebuilding and development of their ancestral homes.

The García Naveira brothers, Betanzos (Wikipedia)

As ever, those who succeeded in life and returned home sometimes went to great lengths to show the loveliness of all that they had left behind in Argentina.

Others, such as the entrepreneur brothers Juan María and Jesús García Naveira, returned to Betanzos in the early twentieth century with considerable wealth and even greater generosity. What they had they shared. Together and individually, they spent their fortunes in providing support for anybody who was sick, disabled, poor or simply struggling to make ends meet. They built schools, a recreation area and a laundry.

When the brothers died, the grateful people of Betanzos erected a statue and constructed a magnificent public square in their honour. It is not surprising that pilgrims discover that their Camino leads them across the square and past the tangible reminder that compassion was not only needed in days gone by but is also an essential ingredient of life today.

As I make my pilgrimage through Lent, am I willing to share my resources with others? Am I willing to give them my time and attention? Do I notice when others might need help? How compassionate am I this Lent?

GOSPEL REFLECTION

"The greatest among you will be your servant."

Matthew 23:11

PRAYER

Dearest Jesus, teach me to be generous. Teach me to serve you as you deserve: to give and not to count the cost, to fight and not to heed the wounds, to toil and not to seek for rest, to labour and not to ask for reward, save that of knowing that I do your will.

St Ignatius Loyola

DAY 15: THE GOD WHO WORKS WONDERS

Wednesday of the second week of Lent

He doesn't look like the traditional picture of an angel. There are no wings, no halo and no bright lights. In fact, the statue of the Angel Gabriel is remarkably like countless images of countless saints sculpted during the fourteenth century. His identity is clear because of his closeness to a sculpture of a newly pregnant Mary whose left hand is placed over her abdomen to draw attention to the new life within her.

Both figures stand in their own niche on either side of the church of Santa Maria del Azogue in Bezantos. Neither shows any emotion which might reveal that the greatest event of human history has just happened: God has become a microscopic human embryo within the confines of a woman's womb. Gabriel and Mary are almost matter of fact: Gabriel was sent to ask if Mary would agree to become the mother of God and she said yes. It was a miracle beyond explanation. How could a woman become the mother of the God through whom she and the entire universe came into existence ? And yet there's no great show. Humanity didn't stop in amazement and awe. People continued their ordinary daily lives, oblivious to the wonder in their midst.

Angel Gabriel (Above) and Our Lady (Below), church of Santa Maria del Azogue, Betanzos

The Camino Inglés passes alongside the church, which means that countless pilgrims must have seen the sculptures of Gabriel and Mary in their solemnity and "ordinariness".

How many stopped to reflect that if God could achieve the extraordinary within the ordinary, then amazing things might be happening within their own hearts, unsuspected even by themselves?

Do I allow God to work wonders in me? The mother of James and John hoped that Jesus might give her sons positions of status and authority. All God asked of Mary was a place within her womb.

GOSPEL REFLECTION

Then the mother of the sons of Zebedee came to him with her sons, and kneeling before him, she asked a favour of him. And he said to her, "What do you want?" She said to him, "Declare that these two sons of mine will sit, one at your right hand and one at your left, in your kingdom."

Matthew 20:20-21

PRAYER

Lord, make your home in me as I make mine in you. Amen.

"I LOVE YOU"

Mary's life wasn't divided into compartments, but it's fascinating to see just how many churches in Galicia present a complex nativity scene, perhaps at their entrance or maybe in some other artistic representation within the church. Santa Maria del Azogue in Bezantos is no exception.

Above the main entrance, a fourteenth-century sculpture shows, in one expanse, the annunciation, the Nativity and the coming of the Magi to honour the new-born Jesus. It's almost like a filmstrip in stone: because of Mary's "Yes", Jesus was born. As a result of Jesus' birth, the world came to know him: God in the form of a human child.

*Entrance arch,
Santa Maria del
Azogue, Bezantos
(Wikipedia)*

Pilgrims only travel to Compostela because the Incarnation happened. The shrine of St James exists because people believed – and believe – that there was something special in the message of the Gospel; that it was saying that God considered humanity special beyond the ups and downs, joys and sorrows, faults and failings of the individual. The Incarnation is God's way of saying, "I love you". Pilgrims journey in search of that love, hoping to experience it in their lives, searching for its meaning.

We all need love. As the song says, "Love makes the world go around". Do I believe that God loves me? How can I show my love for God this Lent? In today's Gospel, the rich man has put himself into one comfortable compartment and has left Lazarus in another, out of sight and out of mind. Do I compartmentalise my life and relationships?

"There was a rich man who was dressed in purple and fine linen and who feasted sumptuously every day. And at his gate lay a poor man named Lazarus, covered with sores, who longed to satisfy his hunger with what fell from the rich man's table; even the dogs would come and lick his sores."

Luke 16:19-21

PRAYER

Loving Lord, teach me the meaning of love. Let me never look down on other people. Let me treat them with the respect and courtesy which you would expect of me. Amen.

"YOU ARE BEAUTIFUL!"

The unadorned beauty of the walls and arches inside the fourteenth-century Romanesque church of Santa Maria del Azogue is hard to beat. For sure, there's a magnificent altar and religious statues grace almost every alcove, but the bare walls and

pillars with their sculpted capitals carry their own message. They declare that loveliness – and therefore, God - can be found in simplicity, without any need to pretension.

How many craftsmen and labourers built this church on the foundations of an earlier one? How many generations of families

Santa Maria del Azoque interior

worked together to create and complete their section of the whole? Did children help their fathers and elder brothers break stones which grandfathers and uncles sculpted? In days before health and safety legislation, protective clothing, safety goggles and high visibility jackets, were there many injuries or did people simply learn to avoid risks as they worked? How often did workers slip on wooden scaffolding without the protection of a safety harness? How did people stay warm and dry in bad weather?

Most of those working on the building were illiterate, but the inability to read and write didn't stop them creating a thing of beauty. For many, the construction would be an act of faith in the future because the church wasn't an overnight, rapidly completed project. Started in the second half of the fourteenth century, it was only finished almost a century later, so many of those who worked on it did so knowing that it would be their children and grandchildren who would enjoy the fruits of their labour.

The Camino Inglés runs alongside Santa Maria del Azogue so pilgrims saw the land develop until the church was completed. Perhaps they visited the market in the square. Many recognised that they would never see the completed church and, in simplicity, passed by, knowing that the ascending walls and roof skeleton were a declaration of hope in the future generations who would pray there.

Do I sometimes think that I must be someone I am not if I am to be accepted by God?
Do I lose sight of the fact that even when incomplete and weak, I am still beautiful?
Can I look at myself and others today, and say "You are beautiful!" – and mean it?

GOSPEL REFLECTION

Jesus said to them, "Have you never read in the scriptures:

'The stone that the builders rejected
    has become the cornerstone;
This was the Lord's doing,
    and it is amazing in our eyes'?"

Matthew 21:42

PRAYER

Loving Lord, let me glimpse the loveliness that you see in me and in the people around me. As I travel through Lent, give me hope and faith in the future. Amen.

DAY 18: MAKE TIME, TAKE TIME

Saturday of the second week of Lent

If the church of Santa Maria del Azogue is beautiful in its simplicity, there is nothing which is simplistic!

The statue of Mary, crowned, wearing a white robe and carrying Jesus, who is similarly dressed, is surrounded by fifteen intricately carved Baroque scenes of Jesus' passion, death and resurrection. Simplicity, complexity, story and beautiful woodcarving go hand-in-hand to produce an altar which was intended to be seen and examined in detail for the messages it carries.

There is something different in the main body of the church, which is one of only two known places in the world to have a sculpted stone medieval calendar on its pillars. Amazingly, although these carvings appear to have been carved in three pieces, each is a single block of stone and was, many years ago, painted, colourful and highly decorative.

August-November figures on the calendar on the pillars (Above) The high altar (Below), Santa Maria del Azogue, Bezantos

Apart from January, which features the Roman god Janus, who looked backwards to the old year and forwards to the new, each month shows its characteristic human activity.

February shows someone huddled over a fire, trying to keep warm.

March, the time to start preparing the vines if there is to be a harvest later in the year, is still cold, so the vinedresser wears a hood to keep warm.

July heralds the harvest, so a man walks towards his field with sickle in hand, whilst August is for threshing the grain and September is the grape harvest... and so the year continues.

Pilgrims to Compostela in medieval times often expected to spend at least a year on their journey. The Camino Inglés was an unusually short pilgrimage route. Yet it still needed time, preparation, thought and planning. We still need those today, don't we? Even the six weeks of Lent shouldn't be something which come as a surprise when Holy Thursday appears on the calendar! We still need to make time and take time.

GOSPEL REFLECTION

"When his mother Mary had been engaged to Joseph, but before they lived together, she was found to be with child from the Holy Spirit. Her husband Joseph, being a righteous man and unwilling to expose her to public disgrace, planned to dismiss her quietly. But just when he had resolved to do this, an angel of the Lord appeared to him in a dream and said, "Joseph, son of David, do not be afraid to take Mary as your wife, for the child conceived in her is from the Holy Spirit.""

Matthew 1:18-20

PRAYER

Lord, let my journey towards you through Lent give me new life, purpose and hope. Walk with me. Amen.

THE HEAD OR THE HEART?

He's there again! Even the cross on a church is associated with the Andrade boar lest anybody forget that the family money and influence allowed the church to be built and maintained. Perhaps humility wasn't the most notable attribute of Fernán Peres de Andrade "O Bo"?

Cross on the back of the Andrade boar, church of San Francisco de Betanzos

The churches of Santa María de Azogue and San Francisco, both of which he built, are to be found almost adjacent to each other on a square and with a cross named after him.

The Plaza de Fernán Pérez de Andrade "O Bo", designed to be a meeting place for anybody coming to and from the churches or the market, is still the site of an annual medieval fair during which the people of Bezantos dress in period costume. Their guild activities, artisan stalls in the market, street theatre and music attract crowds as in yesteryear.

"The world's longest journey is between the head and the heart". Whilst Fernán Pérez de Andrade was showing off his power and might, was there also a part of his heart that was making an inner journey towards God? As he built castles, he also constructed churches and a hospital. When he placed a cross on the back of the Andrade boar, was he perhaps saying that although he built the church, it was to honour Jesus rather than himself?

Do I allow myself to be led by my head or by my heart or by a mixture of both? Do I sometimes know in my head what I ought to be doing and saying, and yet, in my heart, I'm conscious of wanting an escape because I don't want to take the risk? What would happen if I were to let go and let God take the lead?

Year A The woman said to him, "Sir, give me this water, so that I may never be thirsty or have to keep coming here to draw water."

John 4:15

Year B Jesus answered them, "Destroy this temple, and in three days I will raise it up." The Jews then said, "This temple has been under construction for forty-six years, and will you raise it up in three days?" But he was speaking of the temple of his body.

John 2:19-21

Year C Then [Jesus] told this parable: "A man had a fig tree planted in his vineyard; and he came looking for fruit on it and found none. So, he said to the gardener, 'See here! For three years I have come looking for fruit on this fig tree, and still I find none. Cut it down! Why should it be wasting the soil?' He replied, 'Sir, let it alone for one more year, until I dig around it and put manure on it. If it bears fruit next year, well and good; but if not, you can cut it down.'"

Luke 13:6-9

PRAYER

Lord, sometimes it is difficult to do as you ask of me. You are so patient and give me the time that I need to find you. Help me. Lead me. Amen.

To serve and not to be served

He was a fourteenth-century Frenchman who travelled to Italy and didn't visit Spain (as far as it is known), yet surely St Roch must be one of Spain's most popular saints. It appears that every church has a statue of St Roch, pilgrim, Franciscan and patron saint of those who suffer from plague and other infectious diseases.

St Roch, pilgrim and patron saint of people suffering from infectious diseases

Really, it isn't surprising that people should pray to escape the ravages of the plague. The Black Death (1346-1353) is estimated to have wiped out up to half of the Spanish population. The plague of 1596–1602 claimed 600,000-700,000 lives. The Great Plague of Seville (1647–1652) killed up to a quarter of Seville's population, whilst at least 1.25 million people died during the plague years of 1676–1685.

Roch was born in Montpellier and inherited great wealth at about the age of twenty when his parents died. He distributed it amongst the poor and transferred his real estate to his uncle. He then became a Secular Franciscan and made a pilgrimage on foot to Rome to visit the tombs of the apostles. He is remembered as giving himself entirely to caring for people suffering from the plague, whether in hospital or in their own homes.

Roch eventually caught the disease himself and, on recovering, returned to Montpellier. There he was not recognised and was imprisoned as a spy for the five years prior to his death on 16 August 1378.

Images of St Roch show him dressed as a pilgrim and carrying a pilgrim's staff. He wears the Franciscan cord around his waist and, on his cape, the seashell symbolising one who has walked the Camino. On his left leg, he shows the sore so typical of the plague. The saint is often portrayed with a dog carrying bread in its jaws: according to legend, when Roch was ill, the dog was the only one to bring him food.

St Roch went out of his way to serve people who were poor and sick, risking his life on many occasions. Am I prepared to inconvenience myself to help people around me who need a little extra help and support?

GOSPEL REFLECTION

And [Jesus] said, "Truly I tell you, no prophet is accepted in the prophet's home town."

Luke 4:24

PRAYER

Lord God, please help me to put myself out to help others even when I am seriously inconvenienced. Amen.

"DON'T SHOOT THE MESSENGER"

Tuesday of the third week of Lent

Gabriel, the messenger of God, church of San Francisco de Betanzos

They knew all about messengers in medieval times. People needed to communicate with each other in the absence of phones and social media, and so they used a go-between. The important role of a messenger was usually safe: there was a difference between the message and its carrier. Even today, we still have the expression, "Don't shoot the messenger", an expression which, although uttered in 1598 in Shakespeare's *Henry IV, Part 2* and in *Antony and Cleopatra*, dates back to ancient times.

People in the Middle Ages didn't need to study theology to know that Gabriel didn't visit Mary on the angel's own account. God's messenger came from God, delivered the most momentous request ever made of a human being and awaited an answer which would, in turn, be relayed back to God. There seems never to have been a thought that Gabriel might end up as a negotiator. God had asked: Mary replied – and Mary, a young girl from Nazareth, became the Mother of God.

Gabriel's role as messenger is shown artistically across Galicia in works depicting the incarnation of Jesus. The angel is shown carrying an open scroll, a sign that God's message has been delivered. That Mary is portrayed in her pregnancy declares that her positive response had an immediate effect for God, herself and the entire human race. Gabriel delivered a word, but then Mary carried the Word, enfleshed within her.

Today's Gospel shows Jesus, the Word of God, as his own messenger: delivering his message of forgiveness above and beyond the call of duty.

Medieval pilgrims to Compostela often made their journey as an act of sorrow and repentance for their sins. They expected to make God's word a living reality within themselves. Forgiveness and repentance are equally important components of our lives today.

Am I a messenger of the Word of God? Is it a reality in my life? Am I prepared to say yes even if God seems to be asking the impossible? Do I carry the Word with me on my pilgrimage through Lent to Easter and beyond? How's my record on forgiveness and reconciliation?

PRAYER

Jesus, Lord, not all the messages I receive are convenient and satisfying, but neither are they always inconvenient or upsetting. Help me to be realistic. May I find you and your word in all aspects of my life. Help me to welcome the messenger even when I don't want to hear their message. Teach me to be forgiving when the occasion arises. Amen.

GOSPEL REFLECTION

Then Peter came and said to him, "Lord, if another member of the church sins against me, how often should I forgive? As many as seven times?" Jesus said to him, "Not seven times, but, I tell you, seventy-seven times."

Matthew 18:21-22

LIFE'S REAL FOCUS

S ometimes it takes little effort for the eyes and heart to be drawn to what is most important in life.

Church of St James, Betanzos

Take the interior of the church of St James in Betanzos, for instance, an important stopping place for pilgrims on the Camino Inglés. At first, the central aisle looks plain and unadorned – and yet, look again. The natural light streaming through the windows into the sanctuary is, at first, the only available light and, effortlessly, the altar becomes the central focus for anybody entering the church. The aisle, with its fluted pillars, arched roof and wooden pews with their reflected light point directly and unerringly to the altar. The altar is the reason why the church was built in the fifteenth century: to allow pilgrims and non-pilgrims alike to gather in prayer and to celebrate the Eucharist. Nothing has changed. The building still acts as a focal point, not for itself, but for Jesus and the people for whom he lived and died.

Do the eyes of my heart automatically look towards God? Do I ever think about and appreciate the amazing fact that my limited body and soul are a living temple for the One who gives meaning to everything?

"Do not think that I have come to abolish the law or the prophets; I have come not to abolish but to fulfil. For truly I tell you, until heaven and earth pass away, not one letter, not one stroke of a letter, will pass from the law until all is accomplished. Therefore, whoever breaks one of the least of these commandments, and teaches others to do the same, will be called least in the kingdom of heaven; but whoever does them and teaches them will be called great in the kingdom of heaven."

Matthew 5:17-19

PRAYER

Open my eyes, Lord. I want to see Jesus. Amen.

DAY 23:
Thursday of the third week of Lent

Stained-glass window, church of St James, Bezantos

AM I A HEAVENLY SIGN?

It's a cascade! The stained-glass window reveals a large seashell from which a smaller one appears to release a cascade of drops of water and rays of light. But look again: the water and light rays come, not from the small shell, but from the larger one.

The smaller shell is almost falling out of the other, which is stable, illuminated and points beyond the limited circumference of its companion. It's perhaps suggesting that its concerns include and extend beyond the bridge towards which the water drops and light descend.

Where is the bridge? It's easy to suggest that it's local, but we also speak of bridges which form an invisible connecting link of communication between people, their hopes and their dreams.

The window tells of pilgrimage and, especially, that of the Camino. It happens to be on the Camino Inglés, in the church of St James in Bezantos, but its message is much wider than the building.

Does the smaller shell represent the individual pilgrim who is part of the universal pilgrimage towards God? Is its movement helping to scatter the living water and light brought to the world by the One who was and is the Light of the world? As the drops of water and rays of light touch the bridge, are they nurturing the connections which already exist or are they creating new ones? Are they doing both?

Could it be that the individual drops of water and rays of light represent individuals, brought to life during their pilgrimage?

Am I one of them? Is my small personal
journey part of humanity's pilgrimage?
Am I more important than I realise?
Am I part of a bridge which closes the gaps
which might otherwise separate people?
Rain and sunlight come from heaven.
Am I a heavenly sign?

GOSPEL REFLECTION

Others, to test [Jesus], kept demanding
from him a sign from heaven.

Luke 11:16

PRAYER

Living water, refresh my soul. Light of the world, come into
even the darkest areas of my life, transforming them into
radiant places of your love. Help me to build bridges. Amen.

DAY 24:
Friday of the third week of Lent

LESSONS FROM MY LENTEN CAMINO

It's intriguing. In the church of St James in Bezantos, a simple, seven-stepped altar stands beneath the intricate, ornate panel with its beautifully carved figures of the pietà and saints. The contrast between the altar and the reredos could scarcely be more marked – and yet there is something else. The chapel is there to be seen, but it is also a place of private prayer, where the Blessed Sacrament is reserved in the tabernacle. A row of six tealights and a box of matches suggest that, when nobody else is around, someone comes to spend time alone with God. Whoever it is has placed on the altar a small, mass-produced, inexpensive statue of Our Lady of Fatima and one of the Sacred Heart. There may be ancient masterpieces above and around the tabernacle, but the unseen pray-er prefers something simpler.

Altar, church of St James, Bezantos

Do those two small statues tell a story which is perhaps known only to the person who put them there? Does someone who spends time ministering to the needs of others, especially those of pilgrims from all parts of the world, also take time to address his own pilgrimage and its discoveries?

Each of us has a personal pilgrimage through life. We've all had our ups and downs, joys and sorrows, successes and failures, family and friends. Parts of our narrative are open and common knowledge whilst some are private and hidden from the world. Our shared identity might not match that which is personal and not for public consumption.

Similarly, someone who is, at one and the same time, a daughter, mother, grandmother, aunt and worker plays a different part in each role. All are true, but they are also parts of a whole which is much bigger than the individual roles.

What are the similarities and differences between my public and private stories? Which brings me closer to God? What is my Lenten Camino teaching me?

GOSPEL REFLECTION

Then Mary said, "Here am I, the servant of the Lord; let it be with me according to your word." Then the angel departed from her."

Luke 1:38

PRAYER

Lord my God, let me love you with all my heart, with all my soul, with all my mind and with all my strength. Then let me love my neighbour as much as I love myself. Amen.

*The Camino route,
Bruma Mesia*

Which path?

Where have I been? Where am I going?
What was it that I was planning to do?

These are the ordinary, everyday questions
that we ask of ourselves even in our home,
perhaps going from one room to another
when a distraction causes a rethink of
direction and purpose.

They are also important questions which
everybody asks on their Camino. Fortunately,
whichever route pilgrims are taking, someone
has been there beforehand to show the
way. Regular signposts and plaques, all
emblazoned with the seashell symbol of the
Camino, point in the right direction. It's not
easy to get lost. From time to time, beautifully
produced maps add extra information.

Whether you are travelling to Compostela
from A Coruña or Ferrol, the roads meet at
Bruma. The wonderfully varied scenery of
sea, cliffs, towns, forests and hillsides are
a constant enrichment – and could be a
distraction. We're all explorers at heart and
we're all tempted to investigate an interesting
street or a particular scenic viewpoint.

It's so easy to stray from the path and miss
the next signpost. Sometimes that isn't a
problem: it's simply a matter of asking one
of the locals for help in re-routing. A Zambian
proverb says that "whoever has a tongue
is not lost in a forest" – but sometimes one
is walking a forest trail and there's nobody
around. Then what happens? "Pride comes
before a fall." To find my way in life often
means recognising that I am in danger of
heading in the wrong direction.

Many footpaths crisscross the magnificent forests on the Camino Inglés. Without the route markings and maps, it would be easy to "take the road less travelled" and lose the way. Occasionally, however, it pays not to strike out alone but to stick to the path which has obviously been trodden many times by others who are following a similar trail towards a similar goal.

Where have I been? Where am I going? What was it that I was planning to do? Where is my ultimate destination and goal?

Gospel reflection

"But the tax collector, standing far off, would not even look up to heaven, but was beating his breast and saying, 'God, be merciful to me, a sinner!' I tell you, this man went down to his home justified rather than the other; for all who exalt themselves will be humbled, but all who humble themselves will be exalted."

Luke 18:13-14

Prayer

Loving Lord, may I be humble enough to ask for directions when I need them and sufficiently caring to help others to find their right path. Amen.

DAY 26: THE HEARTH OF HOME

Fourth Sunday of Lent

Signpost and pilgrim hostel, Bruma Mesía

"The house is old, the trees are bare,
    Moonless above bends twilight's dome;
But what on earth is half so dear—
So longed for—as the hearth of home?"

These words of Emily Brönte, published posthumously in 1850, strike an echo in every heart. It doesn't matter what the place looks like, home is home.

The Camino routes are punctuated by pilgrim hostels of every shape and size imaginable. Unless someone happens to book into one of the numerous pilgrim hotels on the way, the hostel means sleeping in a dormitory, sharing communal sleeping, recreational, laundry, washing and eating facilities, perhaps eating in one of the local food outlets frequented by other pilgrims as well as by the local people.

The Camino is both a personal journey and a collective experience. Pilgrims share their stories, experiment using unfamiliar languages, encounter people who wouldn't normally cross their path, forge new and often lasting relationships and try new things – including food. At the same time, an inner Camino is taking place, one which might be life-changing, opening the heart to undreamed horizons and possibilities.

A pilgrim hostel guarantees a welcome, offers acceptance – and sometimes the most amazing food – and is an overnight "home from home". Everyone knows that they are on a journey and, in the morning, must pack their rucksack and move on towards their next destination. However, they are all heading towards the common goal of Compostela, a target which provides joy, unity and solidarity during their brief encounter at the hostel.

Life offers me many such opportunities. How often do I make the most of them? Do I ever avoid making the effort of accompanying other people and of communicating with them? Do they occasionally stay away from me? Why? Where do I feel most at home?

GOSPEL REFLECTION

Year A Jesus heard that they had driven him out, and when he found him, he said, "Do you believe in the Son of Man?" He answered, "And who is he, sir? Tell me, so that I may believe in him." Jesus said to him, "You have seen him, and the one speaking with you is he." He said, "Lord, I believe." And he worshipped him.

John 9: 35-38

Year B For God so loved the world that he gave his only Son, so that everyone who believes in him may not perish but may have eternal life.

John 3:16

Year C Then the father said to him, "Son, you are always with me, and all that is mine is yours. But we had to celebrate and rejoice, because this brother of yours was dead and has come to life; he was lost and has been found."

Luke 15:31-32

PRAYER

Open my heart, Lord. I want to love Jesus and everyone who is part of my daily life. At the same time, help me to love myself as the person you made me. Amen.

Day 27: EMBRACE CHANGE

Monday of the fourth week of Lent

Past or present, then or now, today or tomorrow, it doesn't matter. We're on a journey and regardless of our enthusiasm or reluctance, we'll never be the same on any two days in our entire lifetime. We change according to our experiences, choices and encounters with other people.

"I know someone who has made the Camino every year for thirty years! Why?" This genuine question came from a tourist guide who includes the Camino Inglés in his list of itineraries. Perhaps only God and the individual concerned could answer that question. Has the pilgrim covered all the possible routes or only some of them? What does it mean to see familiar faces and places once again but from a different angle from the previous occasion?

What are some of the changes I've seen in me and in the people around me? Obviously, there are alterations with age, but what else has happened? What lessons has life taught me? What has filled me with energy and hope?

The Camino through Bruma Mesía

The official said to him, "Sir, come down before my little boy dies." Jesus said to him, "Go; your son will live." The man believed the word that Jesus spoke to him and started on his way. As he was going down, his slaves met him and told him that his child was alive.

John 4:49-51

PRAYER

Lord, may I walk on your paths with you as my guide. Help me to embrace the changes which bring me closer to you. Amen.

DAY 28:
Tuesday of the fourth week of Lent

FORGIVE AND LET GO

Today, a road bridge across the river Tambre leads into Sigueiro. In the fourteenth century, crossing the river would have been more difficult. How deep was it and how fast-flowing? Were there boats available to ferry travellers from one bank to the other or were pilgrims forced to use their ingenuity?

Margery Kempe wrote the first British recorded autobiographical account of a pilgrimage to Compostela when, in 1417-18, she travelled from King's Lynn to Bristol and thence to Spain. The mystic seems to have followed the Camino Inglés for her to approach Santiago de Compostela via the town of Sigueiro. She herself wrote that she arrived in Compostela on the seventh day after leaving Bristol, stayed there for fourteen days and, thanks to "fair wind and weather", returned to Bristol in five days.

Today's bridge across the Tambre, Sigueiro

Statue of Margery Kempe beside the bridge at Sigueiro (© Phil Hopkins)

Sadly, Margery's account leaves out the fascinating details which we would appreciate today. It is possible that she was illiterate and dictated her autobiography. She probably didn't think that people would be reading her story 600 years after her Camino and might be interested to know, for instance, how she crossed the Tambre, especially with the long, voluminous skirts which were customary in her time. The river's rocky banks must have been both difficult and dangerous, especially in fifteenth-century dress. Who carried her luggage across the river and how? So many facts are lost in the course of time.

But that's true of all of us, isn't it? How often does a family member tell a story which you have completely forgotten or you have described an event of which they remember nothing?

Someone once said that a poor memory is not one that can't remember but is, instead, one which can't forget.

Think for a moment. If you were to remember every single negative event in your life, wouldn't you be miserable? Wouldn't you long to forget? Sadly, it's very easy to advise that we should "forgive and forget" but much more difficult to put it into practice. What would happen if, instead, we were to "forgive and let go"? What pains would you like to let go?

Margery's pilgrimage (School of Divinity: Aspects of the High Middle Ages – University of Edinburgh)

GOSPEL REFLECTION

When Jesus saw him lying there and knew that he had been there a long time, he said to him, "Do you want to be made well?" The sick man answered him, "Sir, I have no one to put me into the pool when the water is stirred up; and while I am making my way, someone else steps down ahead of me." Jesus said to him, "Stand up, take your mat and walk." At once the man was made well, and he took up his mat and began to walk.

John 5:6-9

PRAYER

Lord, walk with me, especially when the going is tough. Give me the courage and faith to continue. Amen.

Day 29: Life's Constants

Wednesday of the fourth week of Lent

According to tradition, the Ponte Maceira's origins are in Roman times. Legend says that the escort for St James' body were searching for somewhere to bury him when

a group of opponents to the Christian message gave chase. The story continues that, as they crossed this bridge, it fell apart because of divine intervention, so that James' disciples were saved and could continue to the place now known as Santiago de Compostela.

True or not, at least since the twelfth century, pilgrims travelling to Compostela via the Camino Inglés have crossed the fast-flowing river Tambre by this bridge. They would have included Margery Kempe as she journeyed from King's Lynn in 1417-18.

Ponte Maceira

Although the bridge of Ponte Maceira has been rebuilt and repaired over the centuries, its foundations remain with little or no change. The years have passed. Water levels have risen and subsided according to the weather and the season. People's purposes for crossing the bridge and their costumes over the centuries have varied. Yet there's a solidity and continuity as if it were declaring that it's stood the test of time and will continue to do so. If we use the expression "tried and tested", then surely it applies in a special way in this instance: a river crossing continues the purpose for which it was built and, for as long as it stands, it will continue to fulfil its duties.

57

My life also has its constants. Some faces and places feel as though they have been there forever, moulding and supporting me. Who have been some of the most important people and why are they so precious? Who has been there for me in good times and not-so-good?

GOSPEL REFLECTION

But Jesus answered them, "My Father is still working, and I also am working."

John 5:17

PRAYER

Thank you, Lord, for the people who have supported me during my life. May I be strong for others when the need arises. May I be a bridge which offers them security and hope in situations which would otherwise be a threat. Amen.

Day 30: Do what I can, not what I can't

Thursday of the fourth week of Lent

If the Ponte Maceira bridge is beautiful, the town on its banks is described as one of the prettiest in Spain! People have lived there for centuries, across changing times, politics, needs, development... and yet there is a harmony and permanence in which all the buildings blend in with one another. Of course, the inhabitants of Ponte Maceira will have the same ups and downs as anybody else, but the tranquillity of the surroundings suggests that people are at peace with themselves and with one another. The dam, bridge, houses, church, mills, fields, forest... It's a picture-postcard scenario.

Ponte Maceira

Is the town of Ponte Maceira heaven on earth for the people who live there and constantly welcome pilgrims as they have done for centuries? Although it's not a tourist destination, do the inhabitants, as in many tourist destinations across the world, breathe a sigh of relief during quiet periods and think about fixing their garden fence or cleaning the windows without having to make polite conversation to passers-by?

How many pilgrims have longed for the peace which appears to be endemic in Ponte Maceira? How many of them have made their pilgrimage after, during or in anticipation of turmoil which affects their lives in one form or another? How many have seen the exquisite beauty of their surroundings and discovered peace breaks out in their hearts? Have some psychologically thrown their troubles into the beautiful river Tambre and allowed its waters to carry them away, out of sight and out of mind?

Which aspects of my life fill me with peace and which cause me anxiety? Can I place them all in God's hands, recognising that I can't solve the world's problems? I am only able to do what I can, not what I can't.

Gospel reflection

Jesus answered, "Those who are well have no need of a physician, but those who are sick; I have come to call not the righteous but sinners to repentance."

Luke 5:31-32

Prayer

Lord, let me put my hand in yours. Lead me where you want to take me but stay with me at every step of the way. Amen.

DAY 31: HEDGING BETS

*Friday of the
fourth week
of Lent*

*Millstone and
millstream*

In any rural village, people depend on the weather. They make the most of their landscape as they plan their crops and flocks according to time-honoured traditions and practice. There's a time for everything – and routine is vital. Farmers know when to bring the pregnant ewes closer to shelter and when to release them to fend for themselves; when to plant and when to harvest.

Everything depends on the harvest and the people of Ponte Maceira for centuries have watched the signs of the times as the months passed by. Life became a little easier when the creation of a dam enabled the construction of a mill and the communal grinding of grain.

Yet life was still uncertain. So many factors could endanger the harvest... and so, as has happened throughout the ages, Christian and pagan traditions became entwined. Parishioners attended Mass and then, heading to the mill to grind their grain into flour, also secretly conducted ancient rituals of witchcraft: anything to combat the risks and to provide for their families. Thus, the mill still incorporates the pentacle, the star associated with witchcraft. It wasn't that the villagers were choosing to dabble in evil practices: they merely wanted to keep the forces for evil on their side and to protect their harvest. They didn't have science and agricultural experts to guide them and simply tried their best with their limited knowledge and understanding.

Have I ever cut a few corners, hedging my bets and perhaps performing questionable activities whilst having the best of intentions?

Then Jesus cried out as he was teaching in the Temple, "You know me, and you know where I am from. I have not come on my own. But the one who sent me is true, and you do not know him. I know him, because I am from him, and he sent me."

John 7:28-29

Pentacle (Left)

The mill (Right)

PRAYER

Lord, help me to recognise my limitations and to live to the best of my ability in the light of your love. May my Lenten Camino help me to take one step at a time, trusting in your unfailing love. Amen.

Saturday of the fourth week of Lent

A NEW DAWN

The end is in sight. A new day dawns and, with it, the still-deserted streets of Santiago de Compostela emerge from the darkness. The cathedral is not yet visible and yet the road is leading there. In one way, it's an act of faith: you know that the cathedral exists but you can't see it and it's too early to check that you are on the right road. Nobody is around to ask.

Dawn in Santiago de Compostela

Your footsteps sound loud on the cobbles and, if you were not alone, you would be speaking in whispers. How many people have trodden this street before you? How many will follow the same route during this very day? Some will have, like you, followed the Camino Inglés, but many won't. This is the point towards which pilgrims are converging from twelve or more different directions and from an unknown number of countries. They are of every shape, size, nationality, occupation and purpose for travelling the Camino.

Your own journey has included some encounters with pilgrims and you have marvelled at the tiny rucksacks of a few and the huge burdens of others. How did they carry them? Few seem to have been concerned about fashion and keeping up appearances: comfort has been their priority and yours.

How have the pilgrims changed during their Camino? Have you changed? How? Has there been an important discovery during Lent? Has there been an unexpected event which turned you upside-down, inside-out and back-to-front so that you had to do a massive re-think? What might the dawn hold for you?

Nicodemus, who had gone to Jesus before, and who was one of them, asked, "Our law does not judge people without first giving them a hearing to find out what they are doing, does it?"

John 7:50-51

PRAYER

Lord of light, dawn in my heart. Lead me towards you. Amen.

WHAT ABOUT ME?

It's still early in the morning but you have found the cathedral and are making your way towards its back entrance. You hadn't thought about the endpoint of your path: you simply knew that it was "somewhere" around the cathedral and that if you were to follow the pilgrims, you would find an entrance which might be open, even if it is early.

The Cathedral of Santiago de Compostela from the Praza das Praterías

Small groups of pilgrims are starting to appear. Most are speaking quietly, perhaps from tiredness, perhaps because there's a sense of "journey's end" and its sacredness. You can hear several languages but can't identify them all. You can feel the pilgrims' excitement and perhaps their relief in achieving a long-planned goal filled with challenges which couldn't always be foreseen. For most, this will be the first time that they have been to Compostela and the first time that they have seen the cathedral other than in photographs or on television. Perhaps they watched the film *The Way* before setting off, hoping to glimpse what might lie ahead.

There's a strange sense that everything and nothing has prepared any of you for this moment. What does the future hold? Am I able to make a fresh start or do I continue the same path because it's tried and tested? When I get back to normal, what is normality? The woman in today's Gospel would never again be the same after meeting Jesus – but what about me?

GOSPEL REFLECTION

Year A Jesus said to her, "Your brother will rise again." Martha said to him, "I know that he will rise again in the resurrection on the last day." Jesus said to her, "I am the resurrection and the life. Those who believe in me, even though they die, will live, and everyone who lives and believes in me will never die. Do you believe this?"

John 11:23-26

Year B Very truly, I tell you, unless a grain of wheat falls into the earth and dies, it remains just a single grain, but if it dies it bears much fruit.

John 12:24

Year C Jesus straightened up and said to her, "Woman, where are they? Has no one condemned you?" She said, "No one, sir." And Jesus said, "Neither do I condemn you. Go your way, and from now on do not sin again."

John 8:10-11

PRAYER

Lord, be with me in life's challenges but also give me a spirit of adventure, curiosity and purpose. Amen.

DAY 34:

Monday of the fifth week of Lent

WALK WITH ME, LORD

Even today, pilgrims cannot plan the exact time of their arrival at the magnificent Cathedral of Santiago de Compostela. A thousand years ago, it might have taken years to travel to their ultimate pilgrimage destination and they would arrive footsore, hungry and perhaps with nowhere to stay. Yet nobody would have wanted to reach the cathedral and simply pass by in search of their creature comforts – and so the doors remained open, day and night, so that pilgrims had an opportunity for uninterrupted prayer, however long they might want to remain.

God alone knows how many pilgrims have travelled to Compostela since the beginning of the cathedral's construction in 1057.

Millions. Over the centuries, the building expanded and developed to keep pace with the needs of the people and, as skills and tastes altered, so did the architectural styles vary. Yet, somehow, the result still manages to be harmonious, beautiful – and can accommodate 1200 visitors at a time.

By day and by night: the Cathedral of Santiago de Compostela

In 1985, UNESCO declared the cathedral a World Heritage Site. Those words, "world heritage" are a good description of somewhere which is one of the Christian world's three most important pilgrimage destinations. The others are Jerusalem and Rome.

The heritage of the Cathedral of Santiago de Compostela is not just in its association with St James, apostle and martyr. Instead, the real message is its spoken and unspoken declaration that the pilgrimage which ends in Compostela is just beginning, starting as the pilgrim leaves to continue their journey through life. It's an assertion which is there for the whole world to inherit and transmit through ages to come: that life is a journey. It is not static. We are always on the move towards a closer, deeper, more loving relationship with God and each other. In making the cathedral a World Heritage Site, UNESCO was saying something that went far deeper than any officials ever imagined.

Lent is moving towards its climax in Holy Week. How can I intensify my preparation to celebrate the passion, death and resurrection of Jesus? As my personal Camino looks towards the greatest gift of self-sacrificing love that the world has ever seen, is there some act of love that I can perform today which will tell both Jesus and someone else that I love them?

GOSPEL REFLECTION

Jesus spoke to them, saying, "I am the light of the world. Whoever follows me will never walk in darkness but will have the light of life."

John 8:12

PRAYER

Walk with me, Lord, through the darkest night and brightest day. Be at my side, Lord. Hold my hand and guide me on my way. Amen.

THE ROAD LESS TRAVELLED

St James holds an open scroll on which are written in Latin the words, "Misit me Dominus" ("The Lord sent me"). The sculpture is part of the magnificent Portico de la Gloria through which pilgrims pass into the basilica.

St James, Portico de la Gloria, (Maestro Mateo)

Above James, Jesus sits in glory, crowned with thorns and showing his wounded hands, feet and side. To his right and left are the four evangelists, Matthew, Mark, Luke and John. Angels display the instruments of Jesus' passion.

James followed his master in more ways than one. The apostle who eventually became the patron saint of Spain had an extraordinarily difficult time when he first arrived in the country and attempted to preach the Gospel message. People didn't want to be weaned away from their pagan deities, some of whom had been significant for many generations. The Romans had imported many but, as was their custom, also adopted the indigenous gods and goddesses they found on arrival. They weren't happy when James told them to abandon their religious practices in favour of worshipping the God of Israel and the new Christian religion.

Jesus could have remained in Nazareth, working as a carpenter. James could have stayed with his boats and nets as a fisherman – but they didn't. Jesus had been sent by his Father and, in turn, sent James to proclaim God's love for humanity.

Just as had happened with Jesus, James generated opposition. He felt that he was getting nowhere and was tempted to abandon Spain and return to Jerusalem. Yet he stayed a while longer and began to make an impression. He was arrested and executed when he eventually went back to Jerusalem. Had he remained in Spain, would he have lived to a peaceful old age? Would that have been taking the easy way out? Who knows?

It's easy to take the path of least resistance and to avoid complications which might become uncomfortable. It's hard to stand up for what I know to be right, especially if I am challenging the convictions and behaviour of people who are close to me. Has there been a moment when I have chosen to take the more difficult path, "the road less travelled"? Has there been a moment when I could have made that choice but didn't because I wanted to avoid the complications?

GOSPEL REFLECTION

"And the one who sent me is with me; he has not left me alone, for I always do what is pleasing to him." As he was saying these things, many believed in him.

John 8:29-30

PRAYER

Lord, help me to be brave when the need arises and to stand up for my belief in your love for each one of us. When the going is tough, be with me and help me. Amen.

Wednesday of the fifth week of Lent

THE WAITING GAME

People are prepared to wait. It's amazing! Some of them carry rucksacks. Some have spent several weeks walking for long distances, sleeping in pilgrim hostels and focusing on reaching Santiago de Compostela – and they wait in amicable patience to enter the cathedral through the Portico de la Gloria. An occasional tour guide will attempt to sort out the details of their pre-arranged itinerary. There's no disorder. Whether or not the pilgrims speak Spanish, they obey (most of) the instructions of the security guards who monitor their progress. As they wait, they enjoy the talents of street musicians and take photographs to remind them of their visit. It's all very peaceful and friendly.

Pilgrims lining up to enter the cathedral via the Portico de la Gloria

How long did Judas have to wait to gain access to the High Priest? Did he go to the main entrance of the Residence or did he sneak to a back door? Hoping that neither Jesus nor the other disciples realised where he was, Judas would not have waited in patience as he worried about being caught out. His arrival had been observed and was the latest gossip amongst the servants. The knowing nods and winks of the "I told you so" brigade accompanied Judas' request to speak to the High Priest.

On the other hand, Annas and Caiaphas had time on their side. They could afford to delay Judas' access to their presence. They were like cats playing with a mouse – except that money was all the bait they needed.

Judas was the weakest link amongst Jesus' companions. It didn't matter if he might have had some other motivation driving his treachery: nobody likes a traitor.

For his part, Jesus would soon enter his personal Portico de la Gloria, a wooden cross accessed by a crown of thorns, scourging and a few iron nails. Jesus also played the waiting game. He was fully aware of Judas' weakness. He'd possibly watched him looking towards the High Priest's palace and suspected the plans under consideration. It was a question of "when?" not "if" his disciple reached the point of no return.

How patient am I if I am kept waiting? Do I make the most of my time or do I give in to feelings of frustration and thoughts of all I could be doing "if only…"? If I am waiting longer than I had expected, how do I treat the person who has to deal with me?

PRAYER

Lord, it's not easy to be patient when I'm looking for results. I want answers today, not tomorrow. Help me when I'm feeling frustrated and stop me if I want to snap at other people, especially when they are innocent bystanders. Amen.

GOSPEL REFLECTION

Then Jesus said to the Jews who had believed in him, "If you continue in my word, you are truly my disciples; and you will know the truth, and the truth will make you free."

John 8:31-32

Day 37:
Thursday of the fifth week of Lent

A MOMENT OF TOGETHERNESS

It's quite a thought. Looking at the figures of the brothers James and John on the Portico de la Gloria, where James is speaking and John listening, what are they discussing? Could they be trying to make sense of Jesus' words in today's Gospel? On the surface, Jesus seems to be speaking in plain language, about his glory and its origins. However, he is also talking about knowing God at a deeper level than the disciples could possibly understand.

James and John, Portico de la Gloria, (Maestro Mateo)

In the sculpture by Maestro Mateo, is James trying to be the elder brother, the know-it-all who patiently explains something he doesn't understand to a younger brother who might or might not have more insight? Is John, whose head is inclined in listening, attempting to be equally patient as he recognises their shared ignorance but loves his brother too much to tell him that he doesn't make much sense? Has the sculptor shown a true moment of dialogue? Has he allowed us to take part in the conversation centuries after he put chisel to stone and 2000 years after any such discussion happened? Is he showing us a real moment of brotherly love and togetherness?

With the benefit of hindsight, it's easy to be critical of the disciples' lack of understanding, but would we have done any better? Two millennia after Jesus walked the earth, we're still trying to make sense of all that he said and did. Even the greatest scholars declare that they are only scratching the surface of the meaning and content of the Gospel story.

Yet there is hope for us. An elderly woman once accosted the great Franciscan theologian St Bonaventure after hearing him preach. "Is there any chance that I might one day love God as much as you do?" The saint replied, "Mother, *anybody* can love God more than Bonaventure".

Can I make today an "I love you" to God?

GOSPEL REFLECTION

Jesus answered, "If I glorify myself, my glory is nothing. It is my Father who glorifies me, he of whom you say, 'He is our God,' though you do not know him. But I know him; if I would say that I do not know him, I would be a liar like you. But I do know him and I keep his word."

John 8:54-55

PRAYER

God of my life, be the God of my love.
Amen.

WHEREVER YOU MIGHT LEAD ME

Daniel's is possibly the first sculpture in history to portray a smile. There he is, on the Portico de la Gloria, a young man standing amidst a group of solemn older prophets with a lovely smile that lights up his face. Other sculptors attempted to show a smile but failed: something was never quite right. Maestro Mateo succeeded and Daniel's smile is real and reaches his eyes.

Daniel, whose name means "God is my judge", was captured in his youth and taken to Babylon in approximately 604 BC. Unlike many others in the court of King Nebuchadnezzar, he and three other young Hebrews succeeded in keeping true to the faith and laws – including dietary regulations – despite pressure to incorporate their faith in God with that of the panoply of Babylonian deities. Known for his wisdom and integrity, Daniel was also able to interpret dreams, including those of the king. He foretold good times and bad, and proved to be such a good manager that he quickly rose in importance. This, of course, inspired jealousy and led to false rumours because of which Daniel was thrown into a den of lions. He survived due to his belief in God and fidelity regardless of the consequences.

Daniel, Portico de la Gloria, (Maestro Mateo)

There, on the Portico de la Gloria, Daniel smiles, knowing that his position was unsafe, knowing that his honesty created enemies who would try to have him killed. He knew that he was doing God's work and that was all that mattered. That is why he smiled.

Jesus also knew that his enemies were closing in and that he had little time left to him. He knew the consequences and remained steadfastly faithful to his Father.

Does Daniel set a good example for me? Do I always do what I know to be right or do I sometimes cut corners?

GOSPEL REFLECTION

"If I am not doing the works of my Father, then do not believe me. But if I do them, even though you do not believe me, believe the works, so that you may know and understand that the Father is in me and I am in the Father." Then they tried to arrest him again, but he escaped from their hands.

John 10:37-39

PRAYER

Beloved Lord, my life is yours. Help me to stay true to all that you ask of me, regardless of the difficulties on my journey. Give me the gifts of wisdom and integrity so that I can walk wherever you might lead me. Amen.

DAY 39:
Saturday of the fifth week of Lent

SPREADING NEWS – OR GOSSIP?

A marketplace offers wonderful opportunities for standing around and sharing gossip! It's been the same since time immemorial. Traders have long gaps between sales when, with time on their hands, they share the news with each other and with their customers. If someone wants to start a debate or a rumour, head to the market! That's also the reason why political campaigners, advertisers and fundraisers head to shopping centres.

The roof of the cathedral in Compostela offers a wonderful view of its surroundings. One can see the full beauty of the bells and especially, the Berenguela Tower. There's also evidence, unseen from the ground, of the bird population which makes the roof and the towers their home and *al fresco* dining area.

Pilgrims in the Plaza

The roof is a humbling experience. So much care is needed with every step across its steepness – and then there's the birds-eye view down into the fifteenth-century Plaza del Obradoiro. People are so small and yet each has a story. Each has unique relationships with family, friends, acquaintances, colleagues... For some, there will be an overlap, but for many, people will pass each other in the plaza and may never meet again. It's the only shared encounter in their entire human history – and it's so brief. Yet there's also a sense of tranquillity and common interest, regardless of belief or non-belief, and independent of gender, nationality, age and social status. Complete strangers laugh together and enjoy the music of street performers and continue their separate paths, forgetting, perhaps, that they looked into someone else's eyes in a moment of pleasurable togetherness.

In today's Gospel, people stand and gossip about Jesus. Were they in the Temple? Did they gather in the marketplace? Were they simply curious or were they genuinely searching for him for a different reason – to follow him as a disciple or to arrest him?

Do I ever give in to the temptation to gossip about someone else? What would it take if, every time I heard somebody criticised and put down, I were to offer a positive comment instead? Could I make a difference!

GOSPEL REFLECTION

Now the Passover of the Jews was near, and many went up from the country to Jerusalem before the Passover to purify themselves. They were looking for Jesus and were asking one another as they stood in the temple, "What do you think? Surely he will not come to the festival, will he?"

John 11:55-56

PRAYER

Lord, watch over, protect and bless the people who are part of my life. Help me to avoid gossip and the spreading of false news, especially when it concerns another person. Amen.

Day 40: Palm Sunday

Give God the Glory

Jesus entered Jerusalem on a donkey to the sound of cheers and the waving of palm branches – and many pilgrims enter the cathedral through the twelfth-century masterpiece of the Portico de la Gloria. What a contrast!

Maestro Mateo was possibly nearly sixty when he accepted to sculpt the entrance to the cathedral and so, in medieval terms, was already an old man. Yet his hands created one of the world's masterpieces ahead of the great artists of the Renaissance. Look at the Portico and, standing amid several solemn Old Testament prophets, the young Daniel smiles with a smile which reaches his eyes as well as his lips. The brothers James and John are having a conversation, with James doing the talking and John, head inclined to his right, doing the listening. It's a work of genius!

And on his knees in the obscurity and darkness behind the glorious artistry of the Portico, kneels Maestro Mateo, humbly accepting that he had created a masterpiece but giving the glory to God. Some of the greatest people in life are also the humblest.

Maestro Mateo (Above) © Xacopedia

Portico de la Gloria (Below)

Jesus rode on a borrowed donkey, would use a borrowed room to share his last meal with his friends and, a few days later, would lie in a borrowed tomb. He could have demanded earthly honour and glory – but didn't.

Where do I stand? Do I ever blow my own trumpet?

Year A When he entered Jerusalem, the whole city was in turmoil, asking, "Who is this?" The crowds were saying, "This is the prophet Jesus from Nazareth in Galilee."

Matthew 21:10,11

Year B They took palm branches and went out to meet him, shouting, "Hosanna!" "Blessed is he who comes in the name of the Lord! Blessed is the king of Israel!"

John 12:13

Year C Some of the Pharisees in the crowd said to him, "Teacher, order your disciples to stop." He answered, "I tell you, if these were silent, the stones would shout out."

Luke 19:38-40

PRAYER

I love you, Jesus my love, above all things. I repent with my whole heart for having offended you. Never permit me to sin again. Grant that I might love you always and then do with me whatever you will.

Stations of the Cross

This familiar prayer, taken from the Stations of the Cross, will continue throughout Holy Week, linking a personal Camino with that of Jesus towards Calvary and the resurrection.

DAY 41:
Monday of Holy Week

WARNING BELLS

When do church bells ring? As an old rhyme declares:

"That folk may come to church in time, I chime;
When pleasure's on the wing, I ring;
To speed the parting soul, I toll."

Church bells do not simply tell the time or call people to pray. They are there in times of happiness, sadness and danger. Many have a history. Some have names. Whereas some are small enough to hold comfortably in one's hand, some are so large that a special tower is built to house them, complete with extra strong supports to protect the bell, the church, the congregation and passers-by. Such is the Berenguela Bell, Spain's third largest ancient bell, which weighs an estimated 6,211 kg and is one of the great bells of Europe.

Altogether, the cathedral has 29 bells, scattered between the Bell Tower (14), Clock Tower (2), Museum (2) and elsewhere. The Berenguela Bell today is a 1733 replica of its predecessor which, cracked and no longer used, stands in the cloister to be seen and touched by the countless pilgrims and visitors to the cathedral. It is neither out of sight nor out of mind!

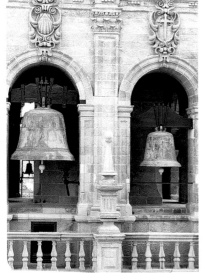

The Berenguela Tower and two smaller bells

Bells have been used since pre-Christian times so, from the fifth century, in adopting their chimes, the Church has merely appropriated something which was already part of life and culture.

Bells don't ring in Holy Week, except on Holy Thursday, when they ring loud and long during the Mass of the Lord's Supper and then fall silent until Easter Sunday morning.

Holy Week is such a special time on my Camino. It's a time to fall silent from time to time so that I can watch and pray with Jesus. What were his thoughts after his entry into Jerusalem on the back of a donkey? When he woke up on Monday morning? Was there a sense of anti climax or of a gathering storm? He knew that the authorities were fully aware of his reception and the fact that people had called him "Messiah". There must have been warning bells sounding in his brain. How did he carry on as normal when normal no longer existed for him?

What will be my normality this week?

GOSPEL REFLECTION

When the great crowd of the Jews learned that he was there, they came not only because of Jesus but also to see Lazarus, whom he had raised from the dead. So the chief priests planned to put Lazarus to death as well, since it was on account of him that many of the Jews were deserting and were believing in Jesus.

John 12:9-11

PRAYER

I love you, Jesus my love, above all things. I repent with my whole heart for having offended you. Never permit me to sin again. Grant that I might love you always and then do with me whatever you will.

Stations of the Cross

*Tuesday of
Holy Week*

SPEND TIME WITH JESUS

Many of us are used to seeing a priest or deacon tip a small amount of incense onto the hot charcoal in a thurible, causing clouds of incense to rise. However, the 80-kg thurible (Botafumeiro) in the Cathedral of Santiago de Compostela dwarfs its small parish counterpart, especially with the weight of incense required for its full effects to be seen.

There's also a difference between the young parish altar server swinging the thurible and the eight red-robed *tiraboleiros* (thurifers) who pull the ropes of the Botafumeiro to swing it above and towards the altar, priest and congregation in the mighty cathedral. The Botafumeiro reaches a height of 21m after about eighty seconds of swinging from its pulley in a 65-m arc and today continues a tradition which possibly began in Compostela during the eleventh century.

*Botafumeiro,
Santiago de
Compostela*

The use of incense in worship predates Christianity by many centuries and is found in numerous ancient cultural traditions. Its sweet smell disguised the not-so-sweet fragrance of sacrifices and holocausts whilst the smoke helped to keep away the insects. It was not long, however, before the smoke held a symbolic importance as representing prayers rising to God from the worshippers below. Because of its association with prayer, incense was – and is – also used to create a calm, prayerful atmosphere.

Jesus was familiar with the incense which filled the Temple. It was used to glorify God – and yet God, in Jesus, stood unseen in the midst of the worshippers. Whilst the priests conducted the many daily sacrifices and burned incense, Jesus probably didn't think that their actions were directed towards himself. Of one thing Jesus was certain: when he entered the Temple on what we call Holy Week, he knew that his time was running out. He had criticised the Jewish authorities too often and, instead of concentrating on animal sacrifices, they were out for the blood of Jesus – and the sooner the better as far as they were concerned.

My Lenten Camino is also heading towards its Easter climax. Am I ready to put my heart and soul into the days that lie ahead? Am I distracted by all the jobs which need my attention or am I able to make a small space in my busy timetable so that I can spend some time with Jesus in his own fear and anxiety?

GOSPEL REFLECTION

"Little children, I am with you only a little longer. You will look for me; and as I said to the Jews so now, I say to you, 'Where I am going, you cannot come.'"

Simon Peter said to him, "Lord, where are you going?" Jesus answered, "Where I am going, you cannot follow me now; but you will follow afterwards." Peter said to him, "Lord, why can I not follow you now? I will lay down my life for you." Jesus answered, "Will you lay down your life for me? Very truly, I tell you, before the cock crows, you will have denied me three times."

John 13: 33. 36-38

PRAYER

I love you, Jesus my love, above all things. I repent with my whole heart for having offended you. Never permit me to sin again. Grant that I might love you always and then do with me whatever you will.

Stations of the Cross

DAY 43: Wednesday of Holy Week

GATHERING CLOUDS

Nuestra Señora de la Barca: Our Lady of the Boat. The small church overlooks the Atlantic Ocean on the Galician coast in north-western Spain. Unprotected from the weather and surrounded by bare rocks, it is

La Señora della Barca

where, according to legend, a frustrated St James wanted to abandon his efforts to preach the Gospel to people who refused to listen. Suddenly, he saw Our Lady, crossing the sea towards him in a stone boat. Mary consoled the unhappy apostle and told him to keep working for her Son. James obeyed – and stayed for forty years.

The extremely hazardous shore surrounding the church is strewn with massive rocks, many of them hidden by the sea, even at low tide. Countless wrecks over the centuries led to the construction of a string of lighthouses to warn anybody travelling by boat.

Because Mary had herself travelled by boat, she became the patroness of the local fishermen and then of seafarers.

Today, the clouds are gathering for Jesus. The storm is approaching.

What storms have I faced in life? How has Jesus helped me? Have I found courage in Mary's example as she followed her Son to Calvary and beyond?

GOSPEL REFLECTION

Then one of the twelve, who was called Judas Iscariot, went to the chief priests and said, "What will you give me if I betray him to you?" They paid him thirty pieces of silver. And from that moment he began to look for an opportunity to betray him.

Matthew 26:14-15

PRAYER

I love you, Jesus my love, above all things. I repent with my whole heart for having offended you. Never permit me to sin again. Grant that I might love you always and then do with me whatever you will.

Stations of the Cross

"Not my will but yours be done"

I n the early days of Christianity, when people were still evading persecution and gathering in catacombs, they celebrated the Eucharist over a martyr's tomb and later on an altar constructed over it. The first dedicated church buildings began to appear during the reign of the Emperor Constantine, as his mother, St Helena, christianised and rebuilt many former pagan temples as churches. However, the altar always remained directly above the martyr's remains. That is why, despite the passage of many centuries, the High Altar in the Cathedral of Santiago de Compostela is directly above what are held by many to be the remains of St James and his two companions, Theodorus and Athanasius.

The current Cathedral of Santiago de Compostela was begun in the eleventh century after the Moors destroyed its ninth-century predecessor. Inevitably, as the building expanded to meet growing demands, people did better than their best to honour the apostle with whom their cathedral has always been associated – and so it became increasingly ornate, especially during the baroque period.

The High Altar
(Top)

St James
(Middle)

The Agony in the
Garden (Right)
(Maestro Mateo)

Enter the cathedral and a dazzling gold and silver baroque altar, with all its complex immensity, surrounds the statue of St James, dressed as a pilgrim with his cape and pilgrim's staff. It is surely above and beyond anything that the apostle could ever have imagined or expected for himself.

By contrast, in the small side chapel of the Corticela, in a bare alcove, Jesus kneels in Gethsemane whilst an angel comes to comfort him. "Not my will but yours be done." His words on Holy Thursday, when he accepted the prospect of his imminent arrest, trial, torture and execution, became a prayer offered by countless followers throughout the following centuries.

The ninth-century sculpture portrays Jesus' fear and anxiety as he prays on his knees, "Father, if it is your will, let this chalice pass me by. But, nevertheless, not my will, but yours be done." But the image of the solitary figure in Gethsemane could scarcely be more different from that of his disciple upstairs.

Pain and suffering are a solitary experience even when there are people offering their love and support. We can't know the feelings and fears of another person, although we can have a very accurate idea of their suffering.

On Holy Thursday, Jesus gave us himself in the Eucharist. In return, humanity gave him the Cross.

Jesus, Lord, let me watch and pray with you in your agony. May I be there for others who are alone and in pain of whatever sort.

GOSPEL REFLECTION

Now before the festival of the Passover, Jesus knew that his hour had come to depart from this world and go to the Father. Having loved his own who were in the world, he loved them to the end.

John 13:1

PRAYER

I love you, Jesus my love, above all things. I repent with my whole heart for having offended you. Never permit me to sin again. Grant that I might love you always and then do with me whatever you will.

Stations of the Cross

DAY 45:
Good Friday

THE TWO SIDES OF THE CROSS

Galicia makes an astounding declaration of faith which links Mary inseparably to Jesus. There are more than twelve thousand *crucieros* throughout the province, many of them dating back to the thirteenth century. From a distance, these are double-sided stone crosses rising above a base of three steps. On closer examination, the front is a standard crucifix. The back, however, shows Mary, not Jesus.

It is logical if you think of what it means to be a mother. Yes, Mary stood at the foot of the cross. However, she was more than an observer. As a mother, Mary felt every moment of Jesus' agony. In a very real sense, as Jesus was crucified, so was she, even if she was not physically nailed to a cross.

The two sides of a crucieros

The *crucieros* are, therefore, a unique way of showing the inseparability of Mary and Jesus in the story of redemption. Again, it's folk art proclaiming a very deep theology: Mary is a mother with mothers – and other mothers can identify with her as they share, not only the joys, but also the sufferings of their children. Mary's presence on the *crucieros* declares, "Look! I'm here for you because I've already been there. You and I share a similar experience."

Erected In public places, the *crucieros* are not only a focus of religious belief, but also for the local community. They are meeting places and their steps also offer a convenient seat to the weary. The cross is within the community.

Today, let me spare a prayer for all those people for whom Good Friday is their current personal reality.

After this, when Jesus knew that all was now finished, he said (in order to fulfil the scripture), "I am thirsty." A jar full of sour wine was standing there. So they put a sponge full of the wine on a branch of hyssop and held it to his mouth. When Jesus had received the wine, he said, "It is finished." Then he bowed his head and gave up his spirit.

John 19:28-30

PRAYER

I love you, Jesus my love, above all things. I repent with my whole heart for having offended you. Never permit me to sin again. Grant that I might love you always and then do with me whatever you will.

Stations of the Cross

Day 46:
Holy Saturday

There when she was needed

Women in the Hebrides and Shetlands traditionally knit jumpers for their menfolk. Each household has a unique pattern so that, if the worst came to the worst and the fishing boat sank, the women can identify and bury their loved ones. They know how to wait, patiently hoping that there would not be an empty seat at the table when they serve the next meal. They are the courageous ones who, when tragedy strikes, forge a new life for themselves and their children, comfort and support each other and "keep the home fires burning". Who is braver – the men who set sail in search of fish or the women they leave behind? Is there a right answer?

The women of the Hebrides, Shetlands and Galicia, as with fishing communities across the world and across time, share much in common with Mary Salome, wife of Zebedee and mother of James and John. We know very little about her. She stood at the foot of the cross and watched Jesus die in agony. She helped to prepare his body for burial and was one of the women who, on Easter Sunday morning, wondered who would move the heavy stone from the opening of his tomb.

The Church of St Maria Salome (Interior © Xunta de Galicia)

It was the Sabbath so there was little that they could do, but Mary the mother of Jesus and Mary Salome were also physically and emotionally exhausted. They and the other women probably spent the Holy Saturday together. Perhaps Mary Salome had previously supported bereaved mothers and wives, but how does anybody find the right words to console a widowed mother whose only son has been tortured and killed? How does one offer support when one's own heart is breaking? The knowledge of a common, shared grief makes the difference – and so Mary Salome stayed with Jesus' mother, regardless of how inadequate she may have felt.

The Church of Maria Salome in Compostela is probably the only church in the world to be dedicated to this heroic woman, remembered because of her relationship to her son James, whose mighty basilica is nearby. Perhaps she also deserves to be remembered in her own right, but that wasn't her way. She was there when she was needed and that's all that mattered.

Can I, like Mary Salome, spend today with Mary? Has my life given me an insight into how they both must have been feeling? Can I be there for someone who is hurting? How?

PRAYER

Help me, Lord, to be available when someone needs my help and support. Help me not to be distracted with thoughts of everything else that I should be doing instead. Teach me to be generous with my time and compassion. Amen.

GOSPEL REFLECTION

On the first day of the week, at early dawn, they came to the tomb, taking the spices that they had prepared.

Luke 24:1

Day 47:
Easter Sunday

Alleluia!

The stone cross at Finisterre (Above)

The symbolic bronze boot where pilgrims leave a pebble or a shell (Below)

Many pilgrims to Santiago de Compostela do not finish their pilgrimage there.

Nobody undertakes a pilgrimage lightly: the complexity of travel arrangements, accommodation, physical and mental fitness, the decision to walk alone or with company... These considerations all add to the initial decision to make a pilgrimage anywhere in the world. It's also meant to be a life-changing exercise. A pilgrim must be wanting inner change and to be ready for it. It's a path towards a more integrated, peaceful and fulfilled life.

A Christian pilgrimage is a response to a dual question of "Who do you say I am?" Jesus asks that question of the pilgrim, but the latter also makes the same in return. Thus, a pilgrimage is a journey of self-discovery through finding and deepening a personal relationship with Jesus.

That's why so many pilgrimages to Compostela do not end there: there's an inner need to symbolise the start of a new dawn, a new life, a new beginning – and so, from Compostela, many continue walking for another four days until they reach the rocky coast of Finisterre (Fisterre in Spanish). Finisterre is synonymous with resurrection and Easter Sunday morning.

The magnificent panorama across the sea towards the Atlantic has been, for many centuries, a shipping hazard. Even when the sea is calm and at low tide, hidden rocks can catch sailors by surprise. That's why the harbour hides an uncounted number of wrecks, some of them centuries old. Even their recovery is dangerous.

Yet there is a lighthouse to warn of danger, but also providing hope of life and survival if someone takes notice of the pitfalls.

Over the centuries, many pilgrims have abandoned their footwear at Finisterre to symbolise the new path that they are taking and the new life that is starting. Some clusters of rocks show where walking boots have been burned so that there can be no return to former days and ways.

Yet there are two other symbols. Many pilgrims, when they start walking, carry a small stone or a scallop shell, intending to bring it to Finisterre and leave it behind at the foot of the cross before they discard their boots. A large bronze boot fastened into a rock represents the untold thousands which people have abandoned as they begin their new life.

Today is, for me, a start of my new Camino through life. How am I planning to begin? First, I want to thank God for everything that I have received and for the many insights I have gathered on my way. Secondly, I will take the first step on the journey through the rest of my life. Third, I will wish anybody and everybody "Buen Camino!" as they travel towards our amazing God.

PRAYER

Walk with me, Lord, every day of my life. Let me know your love and let me give you my love. Small as it is, Lord, my heart is yours. Amen.

GOSPEL REFLECTION

Early on the first day of the week, while it was still dark, Mary Magdalene came to the tomb and saw that the stone had been removed from the tomb. So she ran and went to Simon Peter and the other disciple, the one whom Jesus loved, and said to them, "They have taken the Lord out of the tomb, and we do not know where they have laid him." Then Peter and the other disciple set out and went toward the tomb. The two were running together, but the other disciple outran Peter and reached the tomb first. He bent down to look in and saw the linen wrappings lying there, but he did not go in. Then Simon Peter came, following him, and went into the tomb. He saw the linen wrappings lying there, and the cloth that had been on Jesus' head, not lying with the linen wrappings but rolled up in a place by itself. Then the other disciple, who reached the tomb first, also went in, and he saw and believed; for as yet they did not understand the scripture, that he must rise from the dead.

John 20:1-9